To: Andrea
Keep Building
Keep Brighter Kids ♥Veda

Building Brighter Kids
From Kindergarten to College

Veda H. Green

Published by:

Veda H. Green
Chesapeake, VA

Copyright © 2013 Veda H. Green

Book Cover by: Dynasty

Editing by: Be Well Publishing (Robin Devonish Scott-Susan S. Andres, MEd)

All rights reserved solely by the author. This book guarantees that all contents are original and do not infringe upon the legal rights of any other person or work. No part of this book may be reproduced, stored in retrieval system, or transmitted in any form or by any means—electronic, mechanical, photocopy, recording or other—except for brief quotation in a printed review, without prior permission of the publisher.

ISBN: 978-0-615-78340-6
Veda H. Green
Chesapeake, VA
Printed in the United States of America

Dedication

This book is dedicated to my wonderful husband Donald and the three beautiful children we are building together: Kiah, Donovan, and Christopher. I love you all very much.

Acknowledgments

The Dream Givers—The ultimate Dream Giver, God my Father, who designed me with a purpose and plan in mind. You ordered every one of my steps, and I thank you.

My husband, Donald Green—You are the one whom my soul loves. You believed in this dream long before I knew it could ever come true! Thank you for supporting me in every way and for pushing me to finish this book. I love you!

My mother, Minnie Hightower—You pushed me to be my best! For those days you made me spend reading instead of watching TV, I thank you. For the book reports you made me write; they weren't for naught. I love you!

My sisters, Sherry Siler and Valerie Tyger Hazlett—You have both written and published books so, of course, I had to follow in the footsteps of my big sisters. You have inspired me to be my absolute best! Thank you for loving and supporting me. I love you!

The Dream Keepers—You held on to my dream when I couldn't hold on to it myself: Valerie Tyger Hazlett, Barbara

Simmons Saunders, Randall Saunders, Margo Hazzard, Eric Thompson, Tyra Young, and Latoya Zavala.

The Dream Coaches—You mentored and advised me on how to make the dream of this book a reality: Tim Goler, Dennis Ross, Robin Devonish Scott, and Robert Key II.

The Dream Leaders—You live your dreams and inspire me to live mine: Stephanie Whitley, John Calvin Alberty, Sr., Jack Canfield, Les Brown, Dr. Kathie Mathis, Keisha Rivers-Shorty, and Cheryl Pullins.

The Dream Builders—You proofread, constructively criticized, and allowed me to use your expertise in this book: Torrence Simmons, Carla Watkins Thrower, Carole Derry-Bretsch, Barbara Ford Shabazz, Paula Foster, John C. Alberty, Jr., Geshla Windley, and Kristal Audain.

The Dream Believers—You believed in and supported me and sowed a financial seed in my dream. Thank you!

Introduction

I began this book with apprehension because the written word is far more concrete than the spoken word. Although one can't retract the words spewed from the mouth, the effects sometimes are not quite as lasting; after all, only 30 percent of what is heard is remembered. Words on a page are often taken literally and upheld as the gospel according to whoever wrote it.

Often, people ask the question, "Who or what gives the authority to write a book? Who gives you permission to make yourself an expert on a topic?" Would you believe me if I said my mother? My mother, Minnie Hightower, gave me permission to write this book on the day I was born and she named me Veda. As a child, I didn't really like my name. I wished my mom had named me something more mature, such as Carol, Barbara, or Yolanda. What was a "Veda," and where did she get such a name? I wanted to know, so I asked.

My mother told me that my name wasn't randomly selected, but was thoughtfully chosen because of its meaning. Veda means wisdom and knowledge. Wow! From that day forward, I've loved my name, and I've *lived* my name!

This book is a product of who I have become through my experiences and education. Some might say that it's a coincidence, but I believe it was divine foresight. My mother had a *vision* for my life, and it began to materialize on the day she named me.

So, as you read this book, know it is with every good intention that I write. I am both a teacher and a parent, sometimes at the same time! Many days, I have stood before my students and wondered if I really got through to them. Often, I talked to parents about their children, and I got the same response, "I don't know what to do with him." Sometimes, I heard, "If someone would've told me this about my child sooner, then maybe I could have helped her." If either of these responses sound like something you would say, then please listen and heed the words written in this book.

"It Is Better to Build a Child than Repair an Adult."

That has been my motto for many years. When I was in college, I saw those words cross-stitched on a picture hanging in the home office of my uncle, Dr. Joseph Ford (Uncle Joe). At the time, I agreed with the saying, but it wasn't until I graduated from college, earned my Master's in Education, and became a teacher and parent that I _really_ understood how powerful a proverb it is! I hope that after reading this book, you will make every effort possible to build your children. From this book, I want you to gain three **very** important things:

1. I want you to understand the importance of creating a vision for your children's lives so you will know how to guide them to a successful future.
2. I want you to understand more clearly your role as your child's primary educator and the

importance of assuming and fulfilling that role throughout your children's academic careers.

3. I want you to embrace the "gift of discipline" and see how discipline affects your children's development and ultimately their progress in school.

CHAPTER 1—VISION

"It is today that we create the world of the future."

Eleanor Roosevelt

Have you ever driven by a palm reader's business? You probably chuckled to yourself and said, "Now, that's a rip-off!" I would have to agree with you! I don't believe anyone can foretell the future.

But what if, as a child, you could have been given a crystal ball that showed you your future. Do you think you would be in the place you are now? If not, what would be different? Would you have made the same decisions? Would you have chosen better friends, a more understanding spouse, or a more fulfilling career? Would you have gone to college or selected a different major? Maybe you would've followed your heart and opened a childcare center or an animal clinic. Maybe... just maybe...

What if I told you there *is* a "crystal ball' you can use to shape the outcome of your child's life, would you believe me? Would you believe you hold that crystal ball in your hands now and can use it to "predict" your child's future?

That crystal ball is the ***vision*** you have for your child. In essence, the vision is the kind of life you want your child to have and how you want him to contribute to the world.

Definition of Vision

What is a vision? Webster's defines a vision in many ways. A few definitions follow:

- A vivid mental image
- Sight: the ability to see
- The formation of a mental image of something that is not perceived as real and is not present to the senses
- The manner in which one sees or conceives of something
- Unusual competence in discernment or perception; intelligent foresight

Although these are good definitions, they still don't give you a true meaning based on the vision to be created for your child. Below are some definitions I've created to give you a clearer, more concise explanation of vision. I hope that these will help you understand how critical a role you, the parent, play in building your child's future.

- Vision is your ability to see your children for what you want them to be long before they've become who they will be.

- Vision is the ability to paint the picture of your child's future and mold him or her to fit into that picture with positive guidance.
- Vision is creating a path to the future that is clear enough for your children to see so their choices are made based on their understanding of that vision.

In one of my workshops, a mother stood and said, "Don't you think you're influencing your child and impacting his future too much when you impose your vision on his or her life?" I answered, "I sure hope so!"

You see, as parents, our children are given to us as blank slates. It is our job, our responsibility, to pour into them every good thing we can to insure that they will grow up to be positive, productive contributors to our world. The purpose of a vision is to... keep reading!

Purpose of Vision

One purpose of a vision is to identify and reinforce character traits you want to build in your child, even if you don't see those character traits now. Believe me. I know how easy it is to forget their bright future when they're plucking your nerves in the present! That's why it's best to create the vision when you are away from them, perhaps when they are visiting other relatives or away at camp. That way, you will have a more peaceful mindset, and your best most heartfelt desires for their lives will surface!

Another purpose of a vision is to give your child a deliberate path to follow. You know as well as I do that your child will end up somewhere in adulthood and follow some path along the way! Why not a path that will lead him or her to a bright future? Why not a path that can provide great opportunities, wise choices, and beautiful freedom? Do you want that for your child? Yes? Then, creating a vision is the first step in that journey.

What a Vision Is *Not*

A vision is *not* designed to make your children become what you want them to become! If you always wanted to be a doctor, but didn't for whatever reason, don't try to make your child become a doctor. That's not a vision for him, but for *you*!

A vision is *not* a weapon wielded against your child to make him do whatever you want him to do. That nonsense has no place in the vision. The vision simply is a guide to show your son you have thought about his future, and you want him to have every opportunity available to live up to his potential of greatness.

A vision is *not* static! As your son or daughter changes, so may your vision. It can change, but it must maintain its essential purpose of shaping your child's future.

Elements of the Vision

If you were to read any book on self-esteem, self-improvement, motivation, or behavioral change, you would find that each has some tips and strategies for improving each part of the whole person. If you were to ask any psychologist (I actually did) what parts make up a healthy, whole person, she would agree that there are four essential parts. I bet if I asked, you could tell me the four parts too. Let's list them together: **spiritual, physical, mental, and emotional**. A person who focuses to maintain balance in each of these four areas is a well-rounded, balanced person. Isn't that what we want for our children? Definitely!

Well, would you believe these four essential elements are needed to create a powerful vision for your child? Would you believe me if I told you that focusing on just these four areas in your child's life would nearly guarantee his future success? Why? Because when these four areas are strong and healthy, your child will grow into a healthy productive adult who will make great positive contributions to the world! And that, my friend, is a successful person! Isn't that what we want for our children? Absolutely! So, doesn't it make sense for us to have a vision for our children? Absolutely! Then, let's get to it.

The Spiritual Element. Your vision for your children *must* include a spiritual component. Without this vital part of the vision, your children may have a very difficult time achieving their purpose in life. They must be able to identify and connect to a power greater than self to accomplish the vision you create. This spiritual component will be your children's core, center, and realign them when they get off track. It will rekindle their desire to do what is right and remind them of their commitment to the vision.

This portion of the vision is based on your values and beliefs and is crucial because it will inspire your children to tap into the source of power that ties them to your values and belief system. I chose to write that portion of my children's visions based on the Holy Scriptures because they represent my value system. I want them to understand as they read their vision, that they were created for a purpose, not merely to live their lives for themselves, but to glorify their Creator.

The Mental Element. Your children's mental development is greatly shaped by formal education, but as their primary educator, their first teacher, you must understand that education doesn't *start* when they enroll in school; it *starts* at home! From that premise, you can then plant the seeds in their mind that education doesn't *stop* when school does. Impress them to become lifelong learners!

This portion of the vision is designed, not only to guide your child's academic future, but also their overall outlook on the purpose of education and its importance. It is also in this part of the vision that you will want to focus on expressing the importance of fortifying the mind with healthy images, good books, and positive input.

I'm sure you've heard the United Negro College Fund's motto, *"A mind is a terrible thing to waste."* Although that slogan has become a popular cliché in society today, don't take it lightly! Embrace it! In fact, personalize it! *My child's mind is a terrible thing to waste, and the vision I've created for his or her life is a way to ensure that it doesn't happen.*

The Physical Element. The physical component of your vision involves your sharing with your children your expectations of how they should take care of their body. You will encourage them to live a healthy life, practice good eating habits, exercise, and avoid things that destroy the body, such as tobacco, alcohol, drugs, and so on.

I'm sure you know someone who, if she could, would go back and change the destructive behavior that caused her failing health. That someone just might be you! Although you can't go back, your vision for your child can help prevent the same debilitating behaviors.

In this part of the vision, you can share a little about your family medical history and avoiding some predisposed conditions.

If you're anything like me, then you believe the body is a miraculous machine designed to work efficiently and to heal itself through diet, exercise, rest, and stress management. Don't you want your children to have the advantage of practicing behaviors that yield positive results for their body and health? Of course, you do! After all, *an ounce of prevention is worth a pound of cure.*

The Emotional/Social Element. Whereas the spiritual, mental, and physical elements of the vision deal chiefly with your child's personal growth and development, the emotional/social element introduces interactions with others.

You want to make this component of the vision clear because it will have the greatest impact on your children's social development during those critical adolescent years when they are trying to "find" self.

As a parent, you never want your children influenced by negative peer pressure. You want them to stand up to it, resist it, and decide to be an individual. You want them to be a leader! Well, guess what? If you haven't expressed your expectations clearly, they will have a difficult time with that leadership role when it presents itself.

You will also want to address the importance of making good choices and the outcome those good choices bring, especially in relationships with others. Share with them the importance of treating others the way they would want to be treated by showing respect to authority, using proper manners, and doing good deeds.

Talk about marriage now! It may be difficult to imagine your son as a married man. "Not my son!" you say. Not the one who loses his glasses, forgets to brush his teeth, or refuses to use deodorant (oh wait...that's *my* son). Not he! Yes, he! He may someday find his glasses, brush his teeth, conform to using deodorant, *and* choose to take a spouse. If you want him to choose wisely, you'll be sure to write it in his vision.

In this part of the vision, you may want to also include how important it is to give back, to contribute positively to society.

Although the four elements deal mostly with your children as individuals, they must understand that their role and responsibility are to use their time, talents, and tools to make this world a better place. After all, that *is* the crux of our existence.

Now that you have the elements of the vision, you may be wondering how to create your vision for your child. What kind of teacher would I be if I didn't give you some examples?

A vision can be written in a letter, illustrated in a drawing, expressed in a poem, displayed as a collage, even melodiously recorded in a song. It can be presented in any fashion, but it must include the four elements mentioned above. It must get into your children's mind and heart, must be age appropriate, and, finally, must be clear enough for your children to play repeatedly in their head. You want every decision and action to stem from that central vision.

I have three children. My daughter is fifteen, and my two sons are eleven and four. My daughter's vision is written in letterform in Chapter 4 of this book. My older son's vision is a word collage, and my younger son's vision is a short song I sing to him during bath time.

What I found is, yes, a vision must include those four elements, but for it to mean anything to my children, it must also appeal to their personality. It has to stimulate them and mean something ´ them. One other thing I've learneᵈ visions can change in both presentation as time flexible. You may have to add, take away, or rewrite the vision as your child grows.

That makes sense... after all, I won't be singing a ditty to the tune of "Mary Had a Little Lamb" to my youngest when he turns ten. That would be quite embarrassing for us both, don't you think?

CHAPTER 2—EDUCATION

*"Education is the most powerful weapon
which you can use to change the world."*
Nelson Mandela

Have you ever done corny knock-knock
jokes? We all have! Play along with me.

> *Knock, knock. (Who's there?)*
> *Opportunity. (Opportunity who?) .*
> *Knock, knock. (Who's there?)*
> *Opportunity. (Opportunity who?).*
> *Knock, knock. (Who's there?)*
> *Opportunity. (Opportunity who?)*

By now, you've grown tired of this knock-
knock joke, haven't you?

Well, imagine how your children feel when
opportunity keeps knocking, and they
cannot open the door to learn who or what
it is. The adage, "Opportunity only knocks

once" is not altogether true. Opportunity knocks many times, but it might not be the *same* opportunity twice, and because of this, you want your children prepared to open the door, to reap the rewards of that possible once-in-a-lifetime chance.

Don't you want your children to open the door and walk into their future? Absolutely!

The sad part is that, unfortunately, many children, possibly yours, won't be able to open that door because they won't have the skills necessary to seize the best opportunities. Trust me! *All* types of opportunities will knock at that door.

You want your children equipped to *choose* their opportunity, not to merely settle for what circumstantial opportunities are offered. Circumstantial opportunities? Yes! Circumstantial opportunities! Circumstantial opportunities are those opportunities that put us in the position to settle for what *is* rather than what *could* be.

Chosen opportunities, on the other hand, are those opportunities we *decide* are best for us. We all understand in the Forrest Gump way that "Life is like a box of chocolates. You never know what you're gonna get." That is true. We must all play the hand we're dealt. However, when we are prepared to play the game, our odds of winning are better, and the game is more fun.

How do you improve the odds of your child getting chosen opportunities instead of circumstantial opportunities? Your child must value and understand the importance of getting a good education and become a lifelong learner.

Definition of Education

To define education is futile because no definition captures its true meaning. Education means learning, and our children learn in various ways, from different experiences, and in diverse environments. Although I am a teacher and appreciate our educational institutions, I have not believed nor will I ever believe that formal schooling is the only form of education. *But* because your children spend their most impressionable years in school, the focus of this chapter/section is on formal schooling. *Education* is, according to *Dictionary.com*, "the act or process of imparting (giving) or acquiring (receiving) general knowledge, developing the powers of reasoning and judgment, and preparing oneself or others intellectually for mature life."

There is a give-and-take relationship involved in education. Someone must impart or give education, and someone must acquire or receive education. As this relationship grows and develops, you notice there is a goal—to prepare children *intellectually* to live a productive adult life. Intellectual preparation indicates that, along the line somewhere, the people (children) educated are prepared to make intelligent decisions that will allow them to live independently and productively, to contribute positively to society.

I want parents to stop relying on the school system as the sole source of education for their children. My goals are to help you reclaim the role as your child's primary educator (first teacher), encourage you to give your children a love of learning, and implore you to instill in them the value of education.

Purpose of Education

Although having a definition for education is good, it only scratches the surface of what education really means. The meat of education is its *purpose*, and as parents, we must focus on that purpose so we give our children the best possible opportunity to succeed.

The purpose of education is to teach children how to live their lives by developing their mind and equipping them to live as healthy, productive citizens. Why should you as a parent focus on education and make every effort to make sure your child is intellectually prepared? Keep reading. The statistics are overwhelming!

✓ **More than 8 million** U.S. students in grades 4-12 struggle to read, write, and comprehend adequately

✓ Although the Achievement Gap appears to be narrowing only **4 out of 10 (40%)** fourth graders are proficient in math, whereas only **3 out of 10 (30%)** read on grade level, according to the 2011 National Assessment of Educational Progress (www.nationsreportcard.gov)

✓ The National Center for Education Statistics reports that only about **three-fourths (75%)** of high school students graduate in four years and just over half (about 52%) of African-American and Hispanic students graduate at all (www.nces.ed.gov)

✓ **One out of three** of all incoming college freshmen enroll in remedial reading, writing, or mathematics class

✓ Of urban schoolchildren, **60% do not graduate** from high school

✓ In 2012, one of America's top prison companies Corrections Corporation of America (CCA) made a 184 million dollar profit managing prisons and detention centers

Aren't those statistics astounding? Now that you see what is going on with education (or the lack of it) and our children, we must do what we can to prevent our children from becoming statistics. How do we do this? We must take an active part in educating them because it is not the sole responsibility of the school to do that.

Did you know that most developmental learning occurs during the first four to six years of a child's life? Parents and educators only have a fraction of the child's life to get them set up for success.

Let's say you believe your children will get all they need in school when they enter kindergarten. Statistics show that at least 25% of all preschool children are not ready for kindergarten, thus, even after entering kindergarten, many are fundamentally ill prepared. It has also been shown that if a child in first, second, or third grade falls behind in fundamental skills such as reading, writing, and math, it is highly probable that he or she will struggle through the rest of his or her academic life. If the pattern continues, by fourth grade, it will be next to impossible for the child to catch his or her peers.

Let's look at this from a more concrete perspective. I'm a math teacher, so we must look at the numbers. People may mislead you, but numbers never will. Look at this... A school year in most states is 180 days. Children attend school Monday through Friday for about six to seven hours a day. Kindergarten through the end of fourth grade is 5 years x 180 days a year. This equals 900 days total. Our *average* life span is about 75 years = 27,394 days. Therefore, statistically speaking: *The school has only about 3% of children's lifetimes to give them the skills that will affect them for the remaining 97% of their lives. Wow! That's powerful!*

Now, of course, we know that the brain doesn't stop functioning and absorbing new material after fourth grade, but studies show that every new idea, every new bit of information, and every new concept learned throughout life must be linked to prior ideas, information, and concepts learned during a person's formative years. So, doesn't it make sense that we pour as much into our children as possible during their most impressionable years? Absolutely! Working with your child during the early formative years *before* kindergarten will more than double the amount of impact you have on your child's educational development.

At this point, you might be saying, "Oh, no! It's too late! My child is older than that. What do I do now?" Don't panic! Rest assured; it's *never* too late to do *something*. Jump in where you are and start building your child... *now*!

You have this book in your hands for a reason. I'm here to encourage you that you can do something. Don't waste another school year. Take the points in the upcoming section to steer the ship. This book is your lighthouse. You can do it! Ready? Let's go!

The following section covers the elements of education I believe are most important and that *all* children need to move successfully through school, no matter what age. So, don't give up... keep reading....

Elements of Education

Remember the knock-knock joke at the beginning of this chapter? You learned that Opportunity was on the other side of the door knocking but never found out who or what Opportunity was delivering. We never got to the punch line. The punch line is a wake-up punch. Generally, the punch line is funny, but in this case, it is no laughing matter! The *punch* line of the whole "joke" is this... your children will never know what Opportunity is bringing because they won't be able to open the door! Not funny, is it?

But that's the painful truth for so many children who sit in America's classrooms today. Let's not make it so for yours. To do that, we must first analyze the joke a bit!

Who's knocking at the door? Opportunity! Opportunity can be anything from working in a burger joint to a full academic scholarship! We don't know exactly what the opportunity is, but we know that it is either circumstantial or chosen. Which do you want for your children?

OK, what is standing between your children and their opportunity? Right—the door! Your child is on one side of the door listening to the raps of opportunity. Are they soft and unassuming, or are they strong and deliberate? What does Opportunity have for your children? They won't know until they open the door!

Now, what does the door represent? What stands between your children and Opportunity? Take a guess. If you said education, then you are right. What kind of door do you want your child to have? A strong solid one or one that is drafty and flimsy? You're reading this book, so we already know the answer.

Let's continue our metaphor... A good door has three hinges that make it stable and able to function properly. If the hinges are rusted, uneven, or weak, opening the door could be difficult, if not impossible. If there are no hinges, there can be no door, meaning that Opportunity will never be able to knock at your children's door because it doesn't exist!

The door represents your children's education because education, or the lack of it, plays the largest role in determining which opportunities they can take that will most greatly influence their future. The three hinges represent the three factors that largely influence your child's education: **academics, parent**

involvement, **and** **p**
accountability.

Hinge #1—Academics. As a teacher for more than fifteen years in Virginia, I have watched many educational ideologies come and go. I've been subjected to implementing strategies in classroom management, differentiated instruction, cross curriculum content, even music therapy.

But what I've learned is that no matter how anyone seeks to change the educational system, your children should master certain fundamental skills early and quickly to achieve academic success. I have taught math and science in both middle and high school. I have experienced teaching both high- and low-achieving students.

Do you want to know what I discovered was the greatest difference between those who soared and those who didn't? It was not their socioeconomic status, race, or gender.

Unbelievably, their success or lack of it could be traced to the scores they earned on their third grade reading, writing, and math state tests! For this reason, *I believe that every child should have a strong foundation in the following fundamental skills: reading comprehension, math and problem solving, and communication skills.* When your children have a strong foundation in these areas, especially by fourth grade, they can excel greatly!

Currently, in Virginia, we have Standards of Learning (SOL) Tests. These tests are designed to assess not only what children have learned, but also how they can apply what they've learned. A score of 400 is a passing score with 600 a perfect score. Scoring 500 or greater is considered "Pass Advance." My daughter is now in the tenth grade as this book is written, and these were her SOL scores in third grade: 600 on her Math SOL Test and 485 on her Reading SOL Test.

She hasn't been identified as gifted, nor is she one of those "things come easily to" children. She is a typical student who works hard, but most of all, she has a firm grasp on those fundamental skills!

My eleven-year-old son, now in fifth grade, also did well on his third grade SOL Tests. On his Math SOL Test, he scored 480 and 523 on his Reading SOL Test.

Both my children are "normal" in terms of being typical kids. They like TV, would prefer to socialize with friends in lieu of studying, try to figure ways to get more allowance without doing extra work, avoid chores like the plague, and so on. They are in no way, shape, or form perfect, so please don't say, "Oh, you're a teacher so your kids must be more intelligent!" *No*! If your children grasp these key fundamental skills, they, too, will be better, more intelligent, more educationally sound kids!

So, let me repeat the fundamental skills—reading, math and problem solving, and communication skills. These are the foundation on which to build your child's academic success! I will share with you how much an impact these three skills have on your child's education! Let's go!

Hold on just a moment! Commercial break!

Before we go any further, let me clarify something. Simply because a subject isn't mentioned as a fundamental skill doesn't mean that your child doesn't have to perform well in that class. Every class, every subject, whether academic, elective, or extracurricular, is necessary and important to your child's intellectual preparation. So, don't let Shaunna fail PE just because she thinks it's lame and doesn't want to dress out. Consider these classes the screws that hold the academic hinge in place. Having a hinge with no screws is just as bad as having no hinge.

Now, back to our regularly scheduled program...

You have heard the three fundamental skills mentioned above as the 3Rs: Reading, 'Riting, and 'Rithmetic, but I call them **RAW** because they are the raw materials needed to build your child's educational foundation.

Reading includes word recognition and comprehension. **A**rithmetic involves math and problem solving skills. **W**riting incorporates communication skills, both oral and written language. These lay the foundation needed for your child to build academic success.

A child who can read comprehensively, speak and write coherently, and use math skills adequately usually performs better in class, earns higher scores, and enjoys learning new, more challenging concepts.

In contrast, a child who struggles with these three fundamentals usually demonstrates negative attention-seeking behavior, earns lower scores, and develops a complacent attitude toward school and anything related to it. Which child would you like to see yours become? The fact that you're still reading this book clearly answers that question.

3Rs in the RAW

Reading. Reading is not simply identifying and calling out words, but also comprehending what is read, gathering information, and using that information to solve problems. Children must be able to read, comprehend, think, and apply.

As you may have gathered from reading thus far, my areas of expertise are math and science. My friends call me when their kids need 1st place science fair projects or help with linear equations! So, when I began this section on reading, I had to reach out to some of my other expert sources to give you more details. I know that reading is fundamental, but I wanted to give you a deeper well from which to draw.

Enter my friend, Carla Watkins Thrower. Carla holds a Master's of Education, was an Elementary Reading Specialist, has taught reading for more than twenty years, and is the principal of an academy near Washington, DC.

When I asked Carla what she thought was the greatest reading skill deficit among elementary school children, she answered with one resounding word, *"Comprehension!"*

Carla informed me that...

The primary focus of elementary reading teachers had gone from phonics to fluency and back to phonics. Not until a significant emphasis was placed on NCLB (No Child Left Behind) in 2005 did the focus begin somewhat to shift. Teachers found that students could sound out words and read with fluency, but did not truly know or understand what they had read. They (teachers) began using tricks to teach reading comprehension because they themselves did not quite know how to teach it; hence, we began to see reading recovery teachers hired by school systems and guided reading groups being used more frequently. Reading recovery teachers use various intervention tools in kindergarten classrooms where students display deficits in letter recognition and phonics. Reading recovery is also used in upper level elementary grades to help struggling readers with their comprehension.

What do I want you, the parent, to get from this? What is it that I want *you* to comprehend? It is this... Simply because your children can read words doesn't mean that they understand what the words say. When your children read, they must be able to retell the story, infer, draw conclusions, predict what happens next, sense emotions through words and punctuation, and summarize what they have read. This is comprehension!

Why are these skills important? Why does mastery of these skills define a "true reader"? The reason is that many who call themselves readers are merely getting by. Your children deserve to have more than functional literacy. They deserve to experience the fullness of reading.

What is the fullness of reading? It is the ability to take a page from any book and glean information from it, add to it what they already know, and use it all to be successful in school and life.

More than 30,000,000 Americans are *functionally illiterate*, meaning they have gone through life with just enough reading skills to get by in society. Functional illiteracy is a term used to describe reading and writing skills that are only adequate to manage the daily living and employment tasks requiring reading skills on a basic level.

Those who are functionally illiterate can read things such as traffic signs (mostly identifiable by shape), community signs such as bank, park, or hospital, and words used in everyday language and reading. They can sign a document but may not understand what that document means. They function in society, but few seldom reach their potential in the world.

They hardly seek to learn more or stretch themselves beyond their current condition. They see the world as a narrow strip of possibilities and limit themselves to reach only as far as they can see. Many take the road of least resistance, avoiding challenges that would afford them more opportunity. Few develop new ideas or create opportunities for themselves or others.

We want our children to be real readers because real readers are real thinkers, and real thinkers change the world. Of course, there are people in the world who are successful although they are functionally illiterate, but they are exceptions to the rule. We don't want our children to be exceptions; we want them to be <u>exceptional.</u>

Arithmetic/Math. Math is the study of the measurements, properties, and relationships of quantities and sets using numbers and symbols. I can see your face now. If you are anything like my sister, a graduate of "No-Math High," then you are probably no closer to understanding the meaning of math than you were two seconds ago.

Simply stated, math is the relationship among numbers and symbols working together to create a solution to a problem. Addition, subtraction, multiplication, and division are the basic math operations used to govern the world of mathematics.

Many of my middle and high school students hate math because, according to them, "It's hard." I found that to break down that barrier, I often have to tell them, "There are only four things you can do in math: add, subtract, multiply, or divide. The key to becoming a great math student is to master those operations and know when and how to use them."

Many breathed a sigh of relief because they realized that they had learned how to do those four simple things in elementary school. Now, we know that math becomes a bit more complex than these one-step elementary problems, but when you understand that every complex math problem can be broken into those four basic operations, math becomes easier.

So, even if your children aren't great math students now, they can improve tremendously by mastering those four operations and understanding when to use them. It may require some effort and discipline to go back to the basics and build, but it will be worth it in the end.

Your children must master math early in their educational development. Because math is progressive, and it builds on itself year after year, subject after subject, it is crucial that they retain and recall math skills taught from one grade to the next. If they miss key concepts, it becomes very difficult to catch up without focused effort. By the time children reach middle school, they should have the fundamental math skills necessary to carry them through high school.

As I watch my middle school math students struggle, I find they have greatest difficulty in these three areas of math: fractions, multiplication, and word problems. Fractions and multiplication should be taught very early in elementary school. Word problems begin as simple word phrases and sentences, and then build into complex problems that involve a great deal of logical thinking with the four basic math operations.

Of the three key areas I mentioned, I believe the first to learn early is multiplication facts. I have watched so many students fail miserably simply because they haven't committed their multiplication facts to memory. I say that every child by third grade, no later than fourth grade, should know all multiplication facts through 12 (1x, 2x, 3x, 4x... through12x) and all perfect squares through 25 (1 x 1, 2 x 2, 3 x 3... through 25 x 25). They *must* know them by heart.

Others may say, "That's what a calculator is for!" To that, I answer, "Ha! The human mind is much faster than a calculator is, and it has a greater capacity for memory! Moreover, there's no ERASE button for the brain! Once information is stored, it is there to stay to be recalled at any time!"

I have also learned that students who perform poorly in math early tend to flounder in math throughout school. They avoid higher-level math and science courses, score poorly on standardized tests, and circumvent opportunities involving higher-level math skills.

This could ultimately cause them to miss great opportunities for college scholarships, internships, and careers that would otherwise lead to a greater earning potential. For those of you thinking, "My child is planning to go into the military and serve her country. Surely, she can get by without having strong math skills," think again.

A close friend whom I call my brother, Torrence Simmons, recently retired as a lieutenant commander from the United States Navy. When I asked him how math affects those trying to enter the military, he said,

Every applicant entering the U.S. Armed Forces is required to take and pass the Armed Services Vocational Aptitude Battery (ASVAB) Test. This test has a great deal of math on it and requires problem solving and critical thinking skills. Also, many of the technical positions of the military use math to determine whether or not a soldier is promoted to the next rank.

Look at what the ASVAB covers. Of the nine categories tested, at least four test math skills.

- General Science (GS)
- Arithmetic Reasoning (AR)
- Word Knowledge (WK)
- Paragraph Comprehension (PC)
- Mathematics Knowledge (MK)
- Electronics Information (EI)
- Automotive and Shop Information (AS)
- Mechanical Comprehension (MC)
- Assembling Objects (AO)
- Verbal Expression (VE) = (WK) + (PC)

So, no matter which direction your child plans to go, strong math skills are necessary.

But what if Ryan doesn't want a career that uses a lot of math? I say, Ryan doesn't know what he wants yet. You are his primary educator, so you must encourage him to do his best in every subject in school.

I'm not saying Ryan will ever be a math wizard who eats, sleeps, and breathes math. But what I want to emphasize is that math mastery and problem solving skills are still crucial, no matter what profession he chooses.

What if Sharron doesn't like math? Sometimes, disliking math may come from experiencing mathematical difficulties, and it can usually be traced to early problems.

Stay alert, and pay attention to what your children are doing in math class and how they communicate with you concerning math work skills. If it looks as if they struggle with assignments, help them learn the necessary skills. If you can't help them yourself, look into tutoring. They can stay after school for additional help from teachers; you can hire a tutor. Tutoring is even available online to accommodate busy families.

Communication Skills. Communication skills are a set of skills that enable a person to convey information so it is received and understood.

But please don't confuse reading with communication skills. Although reading is a component of communication, it is a one-way street. Information is going in, but isn't necessarily coming out.

My older son *loves* to read, and he will spend hours weekly with his library books. I know he's reading good stuff, but if I ask him about what he's reading, and he can't answer clearly or explain to me what he's read, either orally or in writing, he's not communicating effectively.

Our children must be able to relay information intelligently. Children who can do this tend to perform better in school because they can take what they've read, studied, or learned through class lectures and respond effectively on tests and essays.

Yes, I know. We now live in the Information Age where technology abounds. How we communicate is very different today from just two decades ago. I can remember as a child being excited when the local phone company introduced Call Waiting and 3-way Calling. I could talk to more than one friend on the phone at a time. That was amazing! (Stop trying to figure out how old I am.)

As I write this book, e-mail, texting, Skype, Facebook, iPods, iPads, and Twitter have become a way of life for the average teenager. My eleven-year-old is standing next to me right now begging for a Facebook page! He thinks his life will somehow change drastically if he gets one... *now*! He just *has to* keep in touch with his friends from school, although he sees them every day.

We can "reach out and touch" in myriad ways today without having to see a face, hear a voice, or wait a minute. I believe there is nothing wrong with any of these advances in themselves; in fact, I love texting and enjoy many forms of social media. However, I've discovered that because of this modern technology, many of our children have failed to master

English; they instead have created a "slanguage"!

Here's a text message sent by an 8th grader: *Heyyyy gurl!!! R u comn 2 the dance @ skool 2maro? Mi mom kan piccc u up n drp u off if u ax ur mom 1st.*

OK, you say, "That's just a text message. That's how kids communicate with one another." Right? Yes, that is true but look at this...

Look at this answer to an essay question also by an eighth grader:

Q: Explain how abolitionists impacted the Civil War.

A: *B/c sum of the ppl was tryna keep slaves from gettn free but sum ppl wuz tryna free the slaves. They was called abolishnists. U cud b white n still b a*

abolishnist b/c white and black ppl thot it
wuz wrong to keep black ppl for slaves.

When I read this response, I was appalled! Besides the fact that this student didn't answer the question, the spelling was atrocious! Even in all its atrocity, the spelling, or should I say misspelling, didn't shock me as much as the slang. OK, I must admit that the misspelling of abolitionist shocked me a little, especially because it was written in the question, but using the current slanguage to answer a test question made me cringe. When I read it, I wanted to apologize to every English teacher in the world for this obscenity that has become this generation's language!

We *cannot* continue to allow our children to communicate this way! We must hold them to a higher standard. Do you think any profession would select a representative who could not convey the mission of the company or express his ideas appropriately? Of course not! Now, do you see why it is important for our children to have strong communication skills?

We must hold everyone accountable for speaking correctly. Our media has done a poor job of highlighting those who speak intelligently and apply subject-verb agreement. Our society has made it OK to make millions of dollars on the basketball court, but not use any of that money to invest in an English or public speaking course. We as parents have condoned this broken vernacular by allowing our children to speak incorrectly and to be most influenced by those who speak "their language."

Let's start today to hold our children to a higher standard of communication. Why? Unbelievably, we are judged by our ability to communicate and articulate our thoughts clearly and concisely. Not one American President has been unable to convey a message to gain the trust of the American people. Ask yourself whether you would be convinced to vote for a candidate whose platform issues were good, but whose English was terrible. Every time you heard him speak on the news, radio, or read quotations in newspapers that included poor subject/verb agreement, constant misnomers, and faux pas, would you vote for him? Of course not! Why? Be honest! You wouldn't because you wouldn't think he was qualified or equipped to run this country. So, why do we think our children will be given great opportunities when they speak incorrectly? Trust me; they won't! But if you want to risk your child's future trying to disprove this fact, remember I tried to warn you.

We've covered the fundamental skills I believe have the greatest impact on your child's education. So let's look at the whole picture and see where your child fits into it. Most school-age children take about six classes/subjects in school each day. Below is a list showing what subjects your child may take on any level and which fundamental skills are needed to master each subject:

Math—reading comprehension (used to decode word problems), math, and problem solving.

Science—reading comprehension, math and problem solving, and communication skills.

History/Social Studies—reading comprehension and communication skills.

English—reading comprehension and communication skills.

Health/PE—reading comprehension and math and problem solving.

Elective Courses (Art, Chorus, Foreign Languages, Culinary Arts, Technology, and so on)—one or all fundamental skills can be used in your children's elective courses depending on which courses they take.

The list above is a generic overall list of subjects that will follow your child throughout their academic career from elementary school through college.

Now, do you see how crucial it is for your child to have a strong foundation in those three fundamental areas of reading, math, and communication skills to be successful in school? These three subjects are so crucial to learning that I'm willing to put all that I love on the line as a guarantee that children who struggle in school struggle miserably in one or more of these fundamental subjects, *and* I'm almost certain they slipped through the cracks between kindergarten and fourth grade.

Now, the question some may be asking is this, "How does this lack of skills *really* affect my child's academic future?" Glad you asked! Keep reading...

When children struggle with one or more of these three fundamental skills, at least one of the following behaviors is evident:

1. **Low grades**. They usually score low on tests causing their grades to fall dramatically, sometimes resulting in not being promoted to the next grade.

2. **Low self-esteem.** They often feel inadequate among their peers because they usually don't perform as well academically and seldom receive the praise and

encouragement their "smart" friends do. Low self-esteem can lead to poor choices in other areas to be accepted by their peers.

3. **Negative behavior**. Some students act out negatively to get some form of attention. They usually end up the class clown or go the other extreme to become the class bully. They go for the "some attention is better than no attention" behavior.

4. **Disappearing Act**. Still other students find a way to disappear academically. They don't want to be found out, so they simply lie low and stay beneath the radar so no one will figure out that they're struggling. They are considered "good" kids because they cause no problems in school.

Unfortunately, those kids slip through the cracks because many teachers don't realize that they're academically challenged because they aren't "behavior problems." And if teachers realize your children are lacking academically, they may be less inclined to inform you because they have spent so much time dealing with "behavior problems" that they may not have enough time to get in touch with you. So, your child fails in silence!

Hinge #1 has been manufactured for the door called **Education**, but we still have two more hinges to go if you want a strong and sturdy door.

Hinge #2—Parental Involvement. It's the middle of the quarter, and progress reports have been sent home. With those reports, a letter requesting a parent conference is also included.

Teachers hope that students will return the forms filled out by parents requesting a conference, but usually, the parents who request a conference are *not* the ones we (teachers) need to see. We've probably talked to Natalie, the honor roll student's parents two or three times *before* midquarter. As a teacher, I've heard repeatedly, "Where are Justin's parents?" "When am I going to see Karen's mother?" One of the greatest wishes of teachers is to have parents who are more involved. What do I mean by involved? No, I don't mean the overbearing parents who want to control every move teachers make, acting as if there were strings attached to their hands and feet.

An involved parent not only shows up for the "mandatory" school-related activities such as plays, concerts, and open house, but who also assumes the role of primary educator (first teacher) of his or her child. An Involved Parent (IP) understands the many responsibilities of his or her child's education. Some of these roles include

1. Supporting the child at home and providing an environment that supports learning.

2. Being an advocate for the child by being able to communicate your child's strengths, weaknesses, and learning styles to his teacher.

3. Openly communicating with your child's teacher and administrator so you understand the school rules, regulations, and policies and working with them to ensure the child abides by them.

4. Attending school functions, joining the PTA, or becoming an active member or volunteering when you can.
5. Reading, responding to, and returning all correspondence sent home.
6. Making positive proactive steps toward interacting with the child's teachers and taking the initiative to inquire about the child's progress.
7. Instilling in the child the love of learning at an early age.
8. Teaching the child at home the importance of respecting authority, treating others as they want to be treated, following directions, demonstrating tolerance of others, and so on.
9. Knowing the child's friends and understanding the influence they

have on the child's behavior in school.

10. Teaching your children values that will positively affect their lives.

11. Becoming acquainted with the parents of the child's friends to become familiar with their values to determine if they align with yours.

12. Providing and replenishing school supplies as needed throughout the year.

13. Keeping school records updated with current contact information.

14. Knowing what the child is doing socially (texting, social media, music, and so on).

15. Attending to the physical needs that affect your child's learning, such as making sure he eats healthy balanced meals, bathes

regularly, sleeps adequately, sees a doctor/dentist regularly, and exercises daily.

16. Making sure the child has glasses if he needs them. I added this because I've witnessed it so often. Many children are doing poorly in school simply because they can't see well.

This list is not exhaustive by any means, but a start to make you aware of some things that will influence your child academically. Maybe you're doing these things. Great! Maybe you're not. OK, start today.

I want you, the parent, to get in the game. Knowing what is going on with your child is very important to his education. You are not being nosey; you're doing your job. Parental Involvement is critical. Without it, kids are destined to fail or at best minimally succeed. Yes, there are always exceptions, but remember what I said about exceptions. We don't want our kids to be exceptions, but _____ (you fill in the blank).

This is why I chose to make Parental Involvement Hinge #2. It's in the center of the doorjamb. Parental Involvement supports the other two hinges and makes the door called Education functional. Hinge #1 is Academics, and Hinge #3 is Student Accountability. Parental Involvement, Hinge #2, is the secret to your child's academic success!

Hinge #3—Student Accountability. Hinge #3 took me a while to develop. The first two hinges came together like two perfectly matched puzzle pieces. Hinge #3, however, kept me bouncing back and forth until I met with a very special friend, Dr.

Barbara Ford Shabazz. We try to meet once a month for breakfast, lunch, or brunch (whichever works best for our schedules). We usually spend about two uninterrupted hours discussing our hopes, our dreams, our victories, our defeats. We are both working mothers who try to successfully maintain the delicate balance between career and family while still finding time for ourselves, hence, the monthly sister-to-sister breakfast or lunch or brunch or dinner or dessert or... whatever.

In January 2012 at our first breakfast of the New Year, I shared with her how I was stuck on this section of the book. I just couldn't figure out which way to go. She, the very analytical psychologist, mentioned the "information funnel." She told me to look at education as a funnel.

The top of the funnel is wide, demonstrating Hinge #1, the impact of academics (school system) on the child's education. The middle of the funnel narrows, and it is illustrated by Hinge #2, the impact of the parent on the child's education. The end of the funnel is the narrowest and represents Hinge #3, the impact of the child on his or her education.

Student Accountability! Brilliant! Now, why didn't I think of that? After all, I *am* the educator. Just goes to show that we all need someone. Thank you, Barbara.

If you want children who are successful in school and in life, teach them to be lifelong learners. Teach them the importance of getting a good education and taking every opportunity to learn something new. The earlier you start teaching your children this, the earlier they will embrace learning and grow to hold themselves accountable for their education.

Your children must understand they are going to school every day and are responsible for following directions, completing assignments, respecting teachers, participating in class, and all the other tasks and activities involved in getting a good education. Students who hold themselves accountable are more focused and self-motivated, however, self-motivated children rarely are "self" motivated. They only become self-motivated when they have been "parent-motivated."

We set the standard. We give the expectations. We lay the foundation. Parental involvement supports and cultivates student accountability. Here's how Hinge #2 supports Hinge #3. Students who hold themselves accountable don't do so by happenstance. They are taught by their primary educators (first teachers), by us, their parents.

I have self-motivated students who live with me. One is finishing her ninth grade year and the other his fifth grade year. They hold themselves accountable, understand the importance of education, and value it. That is not something they innately practice. The reason they do is that my husband and I taught them those things when they were younger, and now, we *expect* them to practice what they've learned.

They know that when they get home from school, homework is done first. They push themselves to earn good grades and strive for academic excellence.

They also understand failure is a result of either not knowing or not preparing and that failing doesn't make you a failure. They must learn from their mistakes. I am a bit guilty of pushing my kids harder than the typical parent does because I am a teacher, I see firsthand how children struggle in school, and I don't want that for my kids. Honestly, I don't think you want that for yours, either.

I'm going to let you in on a little secret... *when you have children who hold themselves academically accountable, you won't have the headache of doing it for them.* The more you work on the front end preparing them and setting expectations, the less you have to work on the tail end. My grandparents taught me this one very important lesson about raising "good" kids. I'll share that tidbit with you in the

Discipline chapter. So, do you know what that means? Yes, keep reading!

CHAPTER 3—DISCIPLINE

"True freedom is impossible without a mind made free by discipline."
Mortimer J. Adler

You've probably seen my favorite musical, *The Sound of Music* with Julie Andrews. It's my favorite for two reasons... one because it's a delightful movie with a happy ending and two because my fifth grade teacher, Carole Derry, (now Carole Derry-Bretsch) taught us many songs from the musical.

I remember singing, "Let's start at the very beginning, a very good place to start. When you read, you begin with ABC; when you sing, you begin with do, re, mi." Well, this book is a bit different because the very best place to start is in the middle with *Discipline*.

I know you've read the sections on Vision and Education, but if you truly want those two to work for your children, Discipline is crucial.

Although you are reading Discipline as the third section of this book, I wrote it first because it is the most important factor for building your children into healthy, productive adults. As much as I wanted Discipline to be first, it wasn't possible because my name is VEDA, not DEVA, so Discipline had to be third.

That's OK because Veda means knowledge, and wouldn't you know it... I'm a teacher. Talk about the power of a name! Oh, well, let's get back on the subject at hand. Besides, if you've read this much, the information I've shared so far must benefit you. Right? Good! So, sing with me... "Let's start at the very third letter, a very good place to start. When you read, you begin with ABC. When you build your child, you begin with D." Discipline!

Definition of Discipline

Dictionary.com defines Discipline as both a noun and a verb. Because building children takes work, which means you must *do* something and because verbs are "doing" words, I'm going with the verb definition of discipline.

Discipline (verb used with an object)—to train by instruction and exercise; to bring to a state of order and obedience by training and control.

This definition is a verb that must be used with an object. In this case, the object is your children. Now, wait a minute; don't get uptight! I'm by no means calling your children objects or things, although if they are anything like mine, I'm sure at times you don't know who or what they are. I want you to see that Discipline is an action that must be *done* to someone or something.

Look at the definition again. Read it. Now, underline the verbs in the definition. Go ahead; do it now. I'll wait. How many did you get? Two? Train and bring? Great! Did you count the nouns whose roots are verbs?

Look again. Instruction noun; instruct verb. Obedience noun; obey verb. You also may have missed the words that can be both nouns and verbs: training, exercise, and control. Almost every word in the definition of Discipline is a verb. So, you see, for Discipline to work, *you* have to work! There must be action taken, and the best time to start is *now*!

Purpose of Discipline

You may be asking, "What does she mean by discipline? Does she mean that I should spank my child?"

My answer to that question is... that decision is yours to make. I don't know your children nor to which methods of discipline would they positively respond. But what I will say is that all children must be disciplined lovingly and consistently to grow into healthy, productive adults.

With that said, please understand the purpose of this chapter is not to determine what methods of discipline to use for your child in relationship to correcting inappropriate behavior. However, it is designed to show you how the lack of discipline can affect your child's ability to learn in school and negatively influence his adult life.

For the record, here's a tidbit of information my grandparents, LeCount and Melvene Butler, shared with me, and now, I share with you. Lean in closely so you can hear me. *Children crave discipline.* Their little bodies and minds hunger for boundaries and limits. When we fail to provide them with the discipline they need, they begin to self-destruct, so much so that when they encounter discipline of any sort, for instance, in school, they don't know how to handle it. They resist obeying instructions, respecting authority, and following routines, which in turn leads to academic setbacks, constant disciplinary action, and eventually a total rejection of anything remotely related to school and learning.

This can result in, as my Aunt Nell would say, "A hard row to hoe." She and my mother, country girls, often used that farming phrase to express the consequences of not following directions. That saying alone usually straightened me up quickly because I never wanted to "hoe a row" of anything. Today, I see many children who have the potential to contribute greatly to society, yet create for themselves "a hard row to hoe" because they lack discipline.

I can recall one such child in a math class I taught a few years ago. For protection, (not hers, but mine), we'll call her Dana.

Dana's Destiny

It was the fourth quarter of the school year, and I was called to be a middle school math teacher. I was assigned to teach eighth grade math and Algebra 1. The school building was fabulous with state-of-the-art technology in every classroom. I was excited! I *love* math, and I was ready to share my excitement and love of learning with my students. I went to school ready to teach, hoping I would encounter students ready to learn.

In walks Dana, the polar opposite of the students I wanted to encounter on my first day or any day, for that matter! This young woman was very intelligent but obviously uninterested in school. She scored among the highest in the school on all her middle school state tests, but the grades on her report card reflected no such achievement or ability. When I talked to Dana about her grades and her parents' thoughts about her failing, she replied, "Mrs. Green, my mother doesn't care. I do what I want to do."

When I spoke to her guidance counselor, she informed me that Dana disrupts class, disrespects teachers, and spends much of her school day in ISD (in-school detention).

I really took an interest in Dana, reached out, and encouraged her to look at education to change her destiny. Unfortunately, I didn't spend much time with her. She was suspended for the rest of the school year for threatening to do bodily harm to a teacher. I wasn't the teacher, but do you see why I had to change her name?

I ran into Dana about two years after that assignment. She'd become an unwed mother attending summer school struggling to make it through tenth grade. She shared with me how she wished she had listened to what I tried to tell her.

Dana was such a bright young woman who could've had a very different destiny if she had been disciplined. Can she turn her life around? She can, but she has a "hard row to hoe." You see, your children may be bright and have the ability to do great things one day, but if you don't discipline them, you are setting them up for years of "hard rows to hoe."

Elements of Discipline

Let's look at the definition of discipline again and discuss how failure to discipline our children can lead to their "self" destruction. Let's break it down, shall we? Discipline, you know, is a verb, so let's take action. I am going to take each action and discuss how you can use it to build your child.

1. Training by Instruction
2. Exercise (Practice)
3. State of Order
4. Obedience
5. Control

Training by Instruction means you, the parent, are parenting. You are giving clear directions for your children to follow. You are showing them what to do, not just telling them. This part of discipline takes *time* and *effort*. You can't get tired. You can't quit. You can't give in to peer parent pressure. Yes, peer parent pressure! What's peer parent pressure (PPP)? I'm glad you asked. Let me give you an example or two.

Hearing things such as, "Susie's mom lets her have a boyfriend," or "Jake's dad lets him stay up as long as he wants" is PPP. When you decide for your children based on what someone else (the parents of your kids' peers) does for his or her children, you are giving in to peer parent pressure! Now that I've diagnosed PPP, let me give you the medicine to treat the disease.

Take your children outside and have them look at the mailbox or the address on the house and ask, "Does Susie's mom's mail come here?" or "Do Jake's dad's bills come here?" They'll say, "No." Then, you say, "That's because they don't live here! And guess what? They make no decisions here, either! So you can stop telling me what their parents let them do."

OK, back to Training by Instruction. You must not treat your children like new cadets in boot camp, barking orders at them. You must provide them with clear instructions, an example to follow, and unwavering consistency. Without these, your children will never learn discipline.

The cliché, "Do as I say, not as I do" is a poor example of discipline, and if you choose to make it the foundation on which you build your child, you are making a fatal mistake. Instead, focus on this proverb, "More is caught than taught," and then lead by example.

Exercise means to practice. As you train your children, you must also give them the opportunity to practice what you have taught them. As a math teacher, I can't figure out how a teacher spends forty minutes talking and teaching, but the students spend only ten minutes practicing the concept in class. One cannot master the concept if one isn't given enough time to practice it. Practice solidifies the concept in the student's mind. The more practice, the greater the impression on the mind; the easier it becomes to recall the information later.

Training your children is the same. They must be given several chances to master the "concept" you have taught them. Are they going to do it wrong? Of course! Are they going to botch the details? Absolutely! But to master the concepts, they must practice.

The root word of discipline is disciple. A disciple studies, follows, and emulates the master. But even more, a disciple is can replicate the master in his absence. The disciple is so prepared that even if the master is not present, it's as if he is because the disciple knows exactly what to do. Why? Because he or she has practiced.

In essence, our children are our disciples. Whatever we want our children to know and do when we are not around, we'd better give them plenty of chances to practice when we are.

State of Order means developing routines. We are all creatures of habit. We find ourselves doing the same things repeatedly, and when anything changes, we often find it difficult to adjust. Children are the same way. They crave order and direction. They feel safe when they know what to expect, and they feel the opposite when they don't know what's happening next.

Our children expect us to know what we are doing and trust us to provide them with the next step. Do we always know what we're doing? Of course not! A good way to ensure they feel secure in our abilities as parents is to develop routines for them. Routines at home make it easy for your children to adjust to the school environment. Your children's school day is filled with routines and schedules. If they have order all day in school, then come home to chaos, the child becomes confused. This confusion causes your children to switch back and forth every day and may lead them to switch off completely. And guess which way they'll turn the switch? You guessed it! They'll switch to what they see as normal—what they do at home. Children can't help it. What they learn at home is what they take with them to school. So, if they have no routines at home, they will turn their switch to *chaos*, not *order*!

Obedience means to submit to the command of authority. Obedience is crucial! There can be no discipline without obedience. Children must learn to obey authority, and sometimes, that obedience must come without question. We live in a society where, all too often, children are disobedient, and parents condone it. You must teach your child to obey the command of authority, especially in school. Teach your children to respect the position of authority even when they want to question the person of authority. Their teachers deserve respect simply by virtue of their role. Will they always like their teachers? No. Will the teacher always be right? No. Does this give them permission to disrespect or disobey the teacher?

No. Obedient children in the classroom would cut down tremendously on behavior problems and would greatly increase the conduciveness of the learning environment. In turn, more can be taught, more can be learned, and more children would succeed. Isn't that what you want for your child? Absolutely!

Control means choosing to do right even when it's the unpopular thing to do.
It is imperative that you help your children develop an internal locus of control. A *locus* means a location or a place. An internal locus of control means your kids decide from within based on what they've been taught and what they expect from themselves.

An external locus of control causes children to decide based on external circumstances or on someone else's value system. For example, children generally behave in school because they fear getting in trouble with the teacher or their parents. You may be asking yourself, "Well, what's wrong with that? Don't we want our children to be respectful and follow the rules?" Yes, we do; however, what happens when teachers or parents aren't around? Then, what happens to the decision-making locus? Where does the decision to behave correctly come from then?

Fear of external consequences only last so long. You want your children to have an internal locus of control so they will make the best decisions, regardless of external circumstances.

When children are governed by a locus of control rooted in principles, it will be easier for them to stay focused on what is important, what they value, and what their purpose is. Now, do you see that although discipline is labeled a noun, when it comes to our children, it must be a verb? It requires action to have impact.

Stages of Discipline

As I've watched my kids develop and worked with students and youth groups over the years, I've noticed that discipline changes as children change. They go through what I like to call Building Stages. These Building Stages require different types of discipline. There are four building stages: Personality-Building, Brain-Building, Character-Building, and Trust-Building.

Stage One (Birth–5 years)—Personality Building. Children develop most of their personalities within the first five years of life. During these years, a child's parents are the strongest influence in his life because they love us unconditionally and trust us for everything. We supply their food, clothing, shelter, and security. They are clay on a potter's wheel. We can mold them into artful masterpieces or useless junk. They are in our hands to do with as we see fit.

At this age, children develop their first understanding of boundaries/limits and begin to test those limits. The laws of nature are experienced most during these years, and most skills are learned through the senses. The parents establish the laws of the land. Children learn very quickly the difference between pleasure and pain, and most decisions are based on the pleasure/pain method.

If I do this, and it hurts, I may not do it again. If it doesn't, I probably will. Discipline is best instilled during this building stage by being consistent. C-O-N-S-I-S-T-E-N-C-Y is the *key!* You must not waver, but hold your ground. When you say *no*, mean it, and don't change your mind... *ever!* Don't let your child wear you down by crying, falling out, holding his breath, begging, asking the other parent, calling a grandparent, aunt, uncle, neighbor, the police, CPS, or any other agency designed to "protect" children. These are the most crucial years in helping him understand the importance of being obedient and respecting authority. I'm going to let you in on a little secret.

Lean in so you can hear me. Are you listening? OK, here it goes... (shouting)... if you take the time to discipline during these years, you will have very little trouble keeping your kid on the right path as he or she grows up. That's it! Am I saying you will have no trouble? Not at all, but you won't spend your life pulling tissues out of your purse, pulling hair out of your head, or pulling money out of your bank account trying to fix what could have been prevented with early discipline during these years.

Something Funny

My children are what my friend calls VA children. Yes, they were born in Virginia, but that's not what VA stands for. VA children are "voice-activated" children. They hear my voice, read the tone, and respond accordingly. The reason why they are VA kids now at fifteen and eleven (I'm working on the four-year-old) is that they were TA (touch-activated) children during this building stage.

As I said earlier in this section, this book is not designed to determine discipline methods for your children. However, my husband and I have already determined that the hands-on approach works best for disciplining ours. Pats on the back and pats on the bottom during this stage are well balanced in the Green house.

Stage Two (ages 5–10)—Brain Building. During these years, your child spends most of her waking hours in school and away from you. Of the twenty-four hours in a day, ten are spent sleeping, eight are spent in school, and the other six are divided among eating, afterschool programs, piano, violin, gymnastics, karate, watching TV, and getting ready for bed. How much time does that leave you to influence your child now? Not much, huh? During these years, she's influenced most by her teachers. You will practically have to consult her teacher to enforce any rule or idea that you had no problem with when she was younger.

You're going to hear, "Ms. So-and-So said this," or "Ms. Whoever said that." The sun will rise and set on her teacher, so just embrace it.

Do you know what I did during this stage? I used it as a tool. Enlist your child's teacher to help you instill the character traits in your children that you're working to instill in them at home.

It's funny how, looking back, my daughter absolutely *loved* her second grade teacher, but in middle school, *none* of her teachers were lovable! Ha! I can remember when my daughter was in second grade, and her teacher Ms. J taught her manners. You would have thought I knew *nothing* about manners or etiquette because every other word out of her mouth was, "Ms. J said." "Ms. J said you shouldn't talk with food in your mouth." "Ms. J said you should never put your elbows on the table." "Ms. J said to wait until everyone is sitting down before you start eating." I wanted to tell her to pack her stuff and go move in with Ms. J! And I'm sure Ms. J would have taken her in, chiefly because she was a VA child.

Because your children love their teacher, they will listen to and believe almost anything that woman (or man) says. Now is the time for you to build a good working relationship with all their teachers and discuss with them how they influence your child's future. As I mentioned before, use this as an opportunity to get Ms. Sunshine on your child development team.

During these five years, academic development is strongest. How your children feel about school is usually very positive between first and fifth grades. It is then that their teachers will have the greatest influence on them. Gold stars and smiley faces will get them to do just about anything! So, partner with your child's teachers. Trust me; it will make your life at home much more peaceful.

Stage Three (ages 10–15)—Character Building. *Now*, the next five years are the craziest! These are their character-building years where their friends (Lord, help us) have the greatest influence on them. This is the stage when our parents asked us almost every day, "If your friends jumped off a bridge, would you do it too?"

This is also the stage when PPP is most rampant! So, beware! Buckle up and hold on for the ride of a lifetime. These are the middle school/junior high years. Hormones rage, attitudes are stinky, and report cards can look awful. For five years, first–fifth grade, your sweet angel made the honor roll consistently and never gave you an ounce of trouble. Now, suddenly, grades are not important anymore and that attitude, that *attitude*, makes you want to pull the car over and, and, and... OK, calm down.

Let me help you through this. I have a teenage daughter, and no matter how hard I try to get her to see things my way, the *right* way, she thinks I just don't understand, and I know *nothing*! (Hey, wait a minute! She thought the same thing back in elementary school. Doesn't she realize who I am? Ha!) Do you want to know why your honor student's report card suddenly looks like the lyrics to "America the Beautiful" (from C to shining C)? Here are the profound answers. "My friends don't think it's cool to make good grades," or "I don't want to look like a nerd," or my favorite, "I don't like that teacher!" Now, they have lost their minds, and you want to hurt them badly. Who are these so-called *friends*! When did they gain so much power? How can you take them D-O-W-N? Unfortunately, Mom and Dad, you can't!

All you can do is *embrace it*! Yes, I know. These are the most crucial years for them to maintain good grades and develop stronger study habits. How do you work with that? First, realize that between ten and fifteen, the adolescent brain is more concerned with developing relationships, facial hair, and breasts than decoding algebra problems. The mind is constantly bombarded with thoughts, ideas, and fears related to your child's social life rather than academics. Again, I say, "Embrace it!" You can't change it, but what you *can* do to control the greatest influence in their lives right now is *get involved* and *stay involved*!

Discipline at this age is as vital to preserving your children's future as water is to preventing fire destruction. Without it (discipline), they will go wild and cause all kinds of damage to their future. You can curtail this damage by knowing what is going on in your children's lives and staying on top of their schoolwork. Discipline doesn't stop just because they are too old for spankings and the timeout chair.

Loosening and tightening the parental reins at the right times means giving your children the opportunity to make age-appropriate decisions. In sixth grade, children should be made to shower daily (*please* make them shower daily), but they can decide if they want to take a shower before or after dinner. In eighth grade, they may have thirty minutes of free time in the evening and can decide to watch TV, play on the computer, or talk on the phone to a friend. When it comes to academics, however, there must be a set pattern or routine to follow to keep those grades up, but make it fun! Include some of those social aspects.

I suggest getting with a few other parents and instituting study groups. Rotate houses for homework, with the stipulation that homework must be done while they're there. I tried that with my daughter, and she loved it. I was surprised, however, after a few weeks that she told me she'd prefer to study alone. I got her to do what I wanted by allowing her to do what she wanted. Secret weapon!

Stage Four (ages 15–20)—Trust Building. Yes, we are still responsible for discipline during these years. The good news is this: If you've been consistent during the first three building stages, then you won't go through the three pulling phases I mentioned in Stage One: tissue, hair, and money pulling. Stage Four is the "step back and watch" stage. This stage gives your children the opportunity to demonstrate all you have instilled in them. These are the high school and early college years.

During this stage, you will give more responsibility to them. You will trust them to make wise choices for their future. Now is *not* the time, however, to cut the apron strings or tool-belt loops. They are just testing their wings; they must understand that you, the parent, still own the nest. So, she gets the car, but when she doesn't make her curfew, she loses that privilege. Sure, he can get a part-time job, but if the job interferes with his grades, he'll have to quit.

During the college years, you must pray they'll remember all you've instilled in them. They'll make some dumb decisions (we did), but hopefully, they won't be decisions that permanently alter their future.

Parents must leave the lines of communication open during these years and gently guide their kids without being judgmental. Be open with them, and let them know you made mistakes too. Remind them of chosen as opposed to circumstantial opportunities. Have them read the vision you wrote for them. Pray for them daily. Talk to them regularly. Trust them completely. Then, watch them make their mark on the world.

Oh, let me share another little secret with you. When they have kids, they'll raise your grandkids just as you raised them. You'll be proud all over again.

When we as parents commit to disciplining our children, we not only prepare them to do well in school, but also in life. We provide them with what they need to grow into healthy, productive adults who contribute greatly to society. Discipline is the right key. What is your note? Do, re, mi...

CHAPTER 4—ACTION

"Action expresses priorities."
Mahatma Gandhi

When I was a kid, I loved to watch cartoons. The animated TV shows always captured my attention and kept me laughing outloud (LOL was going on even before texting became popular). My mother would allow me to watch only two hours of TV a day—one hour in the afternoon when I'd done my homework and my chores and one hour of TV in the evening before bed. What I watched in the evening varied, but that afternoon hour was always dedicated to cartoons. I loved Tom and Jerry, Tweety and Sylvester, Bugs Bunny and Yosemite Sam (Oooo, that rabbit!), and many others.

The commercials that came between the cartoons always appealed to the kids. There were commercials for Kool-Aid, candy, toys, and whatever else they could get kids to beg their parents to buy for them. Commercials also promoted safety, health and hygiene, and education, using characters such as Woodsy the Owl and Fat Albert.

I still remember the commercials that starred GI Joe, a real American hero. Although I didn't watch the GI Joe cartoon, I loved the commercials. He would always catch some kid causing some major damage to himself or his community and stop him just before the catastrophe happened. GI Joe explained the right thing to do, and then, the kid looked up to him and said, "Now, I know!" and GI Joe would say, "And knowing is half the battle!"

Although I liked the commercial's message, for the life of me, I couldn't figure out what the other half of the battle was (don't judge; I was a kid). As I got older, I realized the other half the battle was simply this... *doing* what GI Joe told them to do.

Now, it's your turn. You're probably saying to yourself, I have information but I still don't know what to do! Well, fortunately, this isn't a thirty-second GI Joe commercial. This is a guide to help you win the other half the battle. It's time to take *action*! I've provided in this section an Action Plan to help you while you fight on the battlefield. This part of the book allows you to jump and work on building your child. Are you ready? Let's go!

Definition of Action

When I looked up *action* in the *American Heritage Dictionary*, I found about fifteen definitions! Don't worry; I'm not going to list them all here. Action is simply this: the process of doing or performing something. Action is just that... doing something! But you know I'm not going to stop there; I'm going to take this definition a step further and define *action* as "the process of doing or performing something on purpose to get a desired result." You see you can act all day and never accomplish the desired result because you're not acting on purpose and you have no idea what your desired result is.

When it comes to your child's education, you must take the *right* action to get the right outcome. If you want your children to be academically successful and grow up to be productive adults who contribute positively to society, then you have to take action that will guide them toward that end. You have to do more than just put them on a school bus every day or enroll them in a great afterschool program.

You have to be involved by making an effort daily to make decisions and complete actions that will positively influence their future. Your child will not just wake one day and say, "Mom and Dad, I'm ready to be a responsible adult." If it were that simple, every adult we know would be just that. And I know you know *someone* who takes responsibility for nothing! Think about that *someone*; now think about your son or daughter. Do you want your child to be like that person? No? I didn't think so.

The difference between the dictionary definition and the *Building Brighter Kids* definition of action is that you won't just start doing something; you're doing something with an end in mind.

Purpose of Action

The purpose of action is to change your current situation or positively affect your future. It's just that simple! If you don't like your current situation, you must *do* something to change it. For example, if you're not making enough money on your current job, then you get another job. But to get another job, you must take action. You may need to update your résumé, start job hunting, possibly enroll in classes to prepare for another occupation, perhaps send out résumés, so on, and so forth. Just staying at the current job wishing for another, however, isn't going to do anything to change your current situation. That's defined as *insanity...*

doing the same thing and expecting different results.

The same is true concerning our children. We must take action if we want them to be successful in school, successful in life. If you want to change your child's current situation (poor grades, misbehavior, disrespectful attitude), you must take *action*!

If you want to influence your children positively and start them out on the right track from the beginning, you must take *action*. If you want responsible adult children who contribute positively to society and make a great impact on the world tomorrow, then you must take *action* today. Are you ready to take *action*? Yes? Let's go!

Elements of Action

The elements of *action* are simple. Evaluate your current situation. Decide what you're going to change. Take steps toward making that change. Repeat.

The difficult part is to know what to do when. Although my advice on job hunting may or may not change your current situation, I am certain that what I'm sharing with you in this book will positively influence the development of your children. The action plan that you will design based on this book can make a difference *if* you follow it!

Taking Action

Before you get started, you may want to download the Companion Workbook online at www.buildingbrighterkids.com. The tool has been designed to help you build an action plan for your child.

VISION

Start creating a **VISION** for each of your children. This may take some time, but it is worth the effort you put into it. You could write a letter to your child (see the Kiah's vision below). You could create a collage (also known as a Vision Board) with pictures and words that will inspire your child to succeed. I created a Vision Board for my son Donovan. You could create a multimedia vision for your child. If you're musically inclined, you could write a song and make a CD.

You could make a movie clip. There are no limits on how to present your vision.

Start working on your vision for your child *today*. Don't procrastinate; please don't put it off! Don't think it has to be perfect! It doesn't have to be perfect, but it does have to be done. Your vision is the first step in the journey you're planning for your child.

Be sure to include the following elements. The questions and statements below each element may help you while you're creating the vision.

- Spiritual
    - o Whom do I want my child to worship?
    - o In what power do I believe?

- o To whom/what/where do I want my child to go when he needs help?
- o When human power fails, to whom do I want my child to go for answers?
- Intellectual
  - o How do I want my child to use his mind?
  - o On what elements do I want my child to base his decisions?
  - o Do I want my child to do well in school and go on to college? (Say that.)
- Physical
  - o How do I want my child to care for his body?
  - o Be sure to tell him what things you think negatively affect the body and to avoid those things.

- Emotional
  - You can link emotional to spiritual when it comes to having a healthy outlook.
  - You may want to tell her to guard her heart.
- Social
  - Discuss choices here— friends, boy/girlfriends, peer pressure, and so on.

These are only suggestions. You can write whatever you think will positively influence your child most. If your vision makes you a little emotional, then you're doing it right.

Kiah's Vision Letter

Dear Kiah,

On April 18, 1998, God gave to us a beautiful baby girl. You were everything your Dad and I could have ever hoped for. You were an answer to prayer. You were born into a family filled with love, laughter, and life. You were born with a God-given purpose. He designed you to do great things, and He blessed us to take part in preparing you to do just that! There is no one in the world who can do what God created you to do.

You are a brilliant light made to shine for the world to see. You are a precious jewel to be treasured and cherished.

Give no one the permission to rob you of your value. You are intelligent, beautiful, wise, confident, strong, talented, and filled with greatness. It is our prayer for you that you trust God to lead you throughout your life. And whenever you're not sure what you should do, read God's Word. It will always be your best source of truth and will give you clear direction. Hold on tightly to God's Word and never be swayed or shaken from believing that His Word is truth.

Life is filled with choices, and your life will be the sum of all the choices you make. Kiah, choose wisely. Don't make your choices based on what others want you to do—not your friends, not your spouse, not even your parents. Make your choices based on the principles of God according to the purpose He has designed specifically for you. It may not always be easy to make choices, and there may be people who won't agree, but be confident in your ability to make sound decisions for yourself. And if you ever struggle with decision-making, read Proverbs 3:5-6 and Jeremiah 29:11-13.

Take care of the body you have been given because you get only one. Be sure to listen to what it is telling you. Follow the health-simple principles of giving your body what it needs every day. Don't abuse it with alcohol, drugs, or deface it with piercings or tattoos. Remember that your body is a temple, and you are wonderfully made by a Creator who took time to create you.

Strive for excellence in all you do. You came with a clear, sound, and powerful mind. Your brain records everything you put into it through your senses. So be careful what you see, hear, smell, taste, and touch. Fill your brain with information that will lead you to make wise decisions. Study hard in school so you will be prepared to open the door when opportunity knocks.

Kiah, choose Jesus. Make Him your Savior, Lord, and Friend. Make heaven the place to spend eternity. It's nice to live abundantly on this earth, but remember the things of this earth won't last forever. Jesus is coming again soon, and we all want to be together in heaven.

Daddy and I love you very much, and nothing would make us stop loving you. We will love you forever and always because you are our blessing from God. Now, go let that bright light shine!

Love forever, no matter what,
Mommy & Daddy

PS from Mommy... Choose your husband very carefully. This one decision can make your life very happy or very difficult! ☺

EDUCATION

When it comes to your Action Plan for **Education,** you must be diligent and consistent, because now you involve others in building your children. You have to share some of your influence by relinquishing all power.

You will trust others to sow seeds in your child's life, but you are still responsible for cultivation of those seeds. You will remain the keeper of the garden. To do that, you must understand how the school system works, interact with the faculty and staff of the school, and inform them about your child. You must always be present. That means that even when you're not physically present, your expectations are so clear that everyone who interacts with your child feels your presence and knows you are always there. Do you want to know how to make that happen? Of course, you do. Keep reading…

Listed below are some actions you should take before the school year starts and at any time during the school year. Use these as often as you need to remain active and involved in your child's education. Some action points will be implemented early in the school year, whereas others will be done later. Some will be done only once, whereas some will be done periodically. Just refer to the plan from time to time to remind yourself what can be done.

School Action Plan

- If your child will be going to a new school in the upcoming year, say from pre-K to elementary or elementary to middle school, schedule a tour with the school during the spring before school lets out. That way you can see the school in action, which will give your child an idea how school looks in session.

- If you cannot take a tour in the spring, take him to his new school during the summer *before* school starts. Introduce yourself to the school administrative team (principal, assistant principal, guidance counselors, and so on), and let them know who your child is.

- Schedule an appointment with the administrator responsible for scheduling classes and making class rosters. Discuss with him or her your child's educational needs to pair your child with the teacher who will best suit those needs. Be straightforward! Tell the administrator that you want the best teacher on your child's grade level. Ask questions!

- o Why do you think she's the best teacher?
- o How long has she been teaching? (You don't want a teacher who's ready to retire.)
- o Is she passionate about education?
- o How does she handle discipline?
- Attend open house/school orientation. If there is a Q & A time, ask questions, but don't attack the teacher.
  - o Do you team-teach with other teachers?
  - o How long have you been teaching?
  - o Do the students have recess/PE daily?

- o Do you welcome parent volunteers into your classroom?
- Obtain e-mail addresses of your child's teachers and send an encouraging message to let them know that you are an involved parent with expectations of your kids, and you look forward to working with them.
- Schedule a one-to-one PT (parent-teacher) conference at the *beginning* of the school year to discuss your child's learning style, likes/dislikes, and your willingness to be a team player.
- During the conference, get a clear understanding of homework, grading, and discipline policies by asking questions.

- o What is your grading policy? Are all assignments given the same weight?
- o How can I keep up with what my child is doing in your class? How can I best communicate with you?
- Read *all* paperwork that comes home within the first few weeks of school. Fill out necessary forms with the most current contact information.
- Establish an account on the school's website (Edline, GradeQuik, Grade Pro, and so on) to access assignments, grades, events, and so on. Check it frequently. Teachers are usually required to post grades weekly.
- Schedule a day to volunteer in your child's classroom to learn

how things are done. You can do this a few times a year.

- Obtain state objectives and guidelines so you know what your child is learning in school and at what pace he should be learning it.
- If your school district gives standardized tests, download the Released State Tests at www.doe.gov and let your child practice taking them to prepare for the real tests.
- Volunteer at school functions or at least show up willing to lend a hand.
- At the beginning of the year, send a note or a small token to school for the teacher, nurse, and the office secretary thanking them for all they do. Give a gift to your child's teacher during

Teacher Appreciation Week. Be thoughtful! Don't give the teacher a stapler unless it's engraved with her name. It doesn't have to cost a great deal of money. Be creative! Trust me! That gift will go a long way in building good rapport and a good working relationship with your child's teacher.

Afterschool Action Plan

The most crucial time of learning, retaining and mastering information occurs during those first one to three critical hours after school.

Where are most kids during this time? You got it! Kids are either in some kind of afterschool daycare program, at home with you (if you're a work-at-home parent), or if they're old enough, home alone. If your child leaves school and goes to an afterschool program at a childcare center or someone's home, then your child will have a caretaker responsible for her safety and welfare. This Action Plan is for the caretaker during those one to three crucial hours between school and being picked up.

Childcare Provider (CCP)

Ask your Childcare Provider (CCP) the following questions:

- Would you be willing to stand in the gap for me while I'm at work to help my child succeed in school?
- Would you be willing to look in my child's planner/notebook for homework assignments and ask if all the needed materials (books, worksheet, and so on) to get the assignment(s) done are there?

- Can you provide an area conducive for study so my child can do his homework?
- Would you be willing to look over his homework for completion and sign his homework log/planner/agenda saying he did his homework or inform me of anything he missed so we can go over it when we get home?

Provide your CCP with the following tools:

- School's telephone number may be needed in case your child forgets something at school, and your CCP needs to call and pick it up.
- The name of your child's teacher and contact information may be needed if additional information is needed concerning homework assignments. This is only

possible if the teacher has provided contact information other than the school's contact numbers.

If you know in what area your child needs strengthening, be sure to provide extra resources (flashcards, enrichment worksheets, books to read, word puzzles, and so on) for him to work on if he finishes or has no homework. He can work on it in his study time.

If your child comes home after school and you're there, here is the Action Plan for you as the **Parent.**

- Provide a homework area where your child works each day. Have necessary supplies there for him, such as pencils, pens, highlighter, paper, scissors, glue, and so on.

- Check book bag for school correspondence, teacher notes, and so on, and the planner/agenda for assignments. Do this even for middle school students. Remember; middle school students are concerned primarily with their social life so you must stay on top of them academically.

  If your child is in high school, you still have to check in with them. You should still require that they communicate with you concerning their homework, projects, tests, dates, and deadlines.

- Require that your child do more than just what's written in the planner. Example: The planner says, "Do p. 44 #1-5." Don't just look at the work to see if it's done and say OK. Ask questions so he will have to explain to you what he's learning. This will reinforce the concepts and solidify them in his mind.

- Require your child read for a time that is at least twice his age. (A ten-year old should read at least twenty minutes a day.)
- Take advantage of every teachable moment. Make your child think!
- On school nights, don't let TV be the last thing your child sees before he goes to bed.

If your children come home alone, then the **Child Action Plan** must be a routine they follow every day!

- Come in the house, lock the door, and call you to let you know they're in the house safely.

- Have a healthy snack and begin homework immediately—no TV, computer/video games, outside or anything!
Require that homework be done before any of those things are done.
- Do chores. I know that's not academically connected, but developing the habit of "work before play" directly affects academic discipline.
- When you get home from work, take some time to look over homework and *talk* to your kids about what they've learned. If you get home too late, make sure they leave their homework out for you to check. Write a note to your children to let them know you've seen their homework.

Circle the ones they may need to revisit in the morning when they get up. If they expect you to check it and understand that they will have to rise a little earlier to correct any mistakes, they will be prone to slow down and take their time on their homework, which will in turn positively affect their grades.

Now, you're probably saying, "Lady, I work twelve-hour shifts, and my eyes are nearly shut when I walk in the door! If you think I'm checking over my kid's homework when I get home, you're crazy!" My response is this, "Yes! I know you may be tired, but I guarantee you it will all pay off! *It will pay off!*" Remember the purpose of action is to change your current situation or positively influence the future! Taking this action today will positively influence your child's tomorrow!

DISCIPLINE

Children should follow daily routines to build discipline. You, as the parent, should also practice being disciplined. It helps build disciplined children.

Sample of an Afterschool Routine (Middle School Child)

- On Tuesday, change into gymnastics clothes.
- Put shirt/clothes in dirty basket.
- Eat your *healthy* snack and drink water/clean your area.
- Empty/clean out your lunchbox and put lunchbox on the counter for Mommy to pack.
- Show Mommy your planner/binder.
- Do your homework.

- o Written homework (show Mommy to check).
- o Study notes (call Study Buddy to review).
- o Online enrichment.
- Pack book bag/gym bag and put it by the door.
- Go outside (weather and time permitting).
- Practice piano/violin for twenty minutes.
- Dinner/clean area and put dishes in dishwasher.

Sample of an Afterschool Routine (Elementary School Child)

- Wash your hands, face, and change your shirt.
  - o On Wednesday, change into karate clothes.
- Put shirt in dirty clothes.

- Eat your *healthy* snack and drink water/clean your area.
- Empty/clean out your lunchbox, and put lunchbox on the counter for Mommy to pack.
- Show Mommy your planner/binder.
- Do your homework.
  - On Wednesday, go to karate class @3:30 (stay focused on homework).
  - Written homework (show Mommy to check).
  - Study spelling words.
  - Review math facts (ten minutes).
- Go outside (weather and time permitting).
- Pack book bag and put it by the door (*ready* to go).
- Practice piano for fifteen minutes.
- Dinner/clean area and put dishes in dishwasher.

ACTION

- You are not behind! Jump in where you are, and go to work!
- Doing something is always better than doing nothing.
- FOCUS! Follow One Course Until Successful! You may not see immediate results, but don't stop. Stay focused on the vision.
- Enlist support from positive people.
- Make yourself aware of what is going on in your child's life—academically, socially, emotionally, spiritually, and physically. You can never be too involved!
- Be the **PARENT**…
  - **P**erson
  - **A**lways
  - **R**esponsible for
  - **E**ducating
  - **N**urturing and
  - **T**raining

I'VE READ THE BOOK! NOW WHAT?

Now, you may be saying, "Wow! This *is* a great book! I really got a lot out of it! I wish I knew what to do and where to start!"

I'm a teacher, and I never leave my students without a next step, so rest assured that I wouldn't leave you hanging, either. If you want more details on how to create your child's Action Plan, go to my website www.buildingbrighterkids.com. There you will find the downloadable Action Plan workbook, articles, and other resources to help you develop your child's action plan. You will also have access to various educational websites to help you help your children succeed in school.

Always remember... it is easier to build a child than repair an adult, and *Building*

Brighter Kids gives you the tools necessary to become a master builder! Are you ready? Let's go! I'll see you online!

Building Brighter Kids™ wants to do more than make you feel good and give you an emotional high. Our goal is to influence the world of education by providing the tools and techniques that will make a difference for you.

To order this book for your church, school, organization; arrange a Building Brighter Kids workshop or speaking engagement for Veda Green, please visit us at www.buildingbrighterkids.com

About the Author

Veda Green is best described as "Excellence in Action!" She is a gifted motivational speaker, dynamic trainer, passionate teacher, and founder of Building Brighter Kids. She is a mover and a shaker. She speaks with conviction and her message is strong. Veda is known for her remarkable storytelling ability, and she uses humor to captivate her audience. Her enthusiasm is contagious! Anyone who has ever been in her presence walks away feeling empowered and ready to change the world.

Veda holds a Bachelor's in Biology from Norfolk State University, and a Master's in Education from Old Dominion University, both in Norfolk, Virginia.

Veda has taught math and science at middle and high school levels for more than fifteen years. Her experience as a dedicated teacher has given her a platform from which to deliver the powerful message, "It is better to build a child than to repair an adult."

Veda currently resides in Chesapeake, Virginia, with the lover of her soul, husband Donald Green. Together, they are building three wonderful children, Kiah, Donovan, and Christopher. Veda lives by the philosophy of faith first, family second, and career third. In her spare time, she enjoys reading, baking, and keeping in touch with friends.